HEART TALK

Your Roadmap to a Healthy Heart

Dr Yatish Agarwal
Rekha Agarwal

जय विज्ञान JAI VIGYAN
२००४
वैज्ञानिक जागरूकता वर्ष
Year of Scientific Awareness

Rajkamal

Rajkamal Books
1-B Netaji Subhash Marg
Daryaganj, New Delhi – 110 002
Tel: 011-232 74463; 232 88769 *Fax*: 23278144
E-mail: Info@rajkamalprakashan.com

ISBN: 978-81-267-1039-3

First published in the *Year of Scientific Awareness*, 2004
This edition, 2012

Advisors
Dr K.K. Sethi, Chief of Cardiology
Delhi Heart & Lung Institute
New Delhi

Dr Mukesh Goel, Cardiac Surgeon
Escorts Heart Institute & Research Centre
New Delhi

Editor : Manju Gupta
Creative Director : Abhimanyu Sinha
Graphics : Tapas Sarkar, Naresh Sharma
Production : Mahesh Chandra

The authors can be reached on the e-mail at: **dryatish@yahoo.com**

₹ 60

Printed at B.K. Offset
Shahadra, Delhi-110 032

This book is intended not as a substitute for personal medical advice but as a supplement to that advice for the patient who wishes to understand more about his or her condition. Before taking any form of treatment, you must always consult your physician. You should note that advances in medical science occur rapidly and some of the information about drugs and treatment contained in this book may soon be out of date.

Contents

Know Your Risk Score

Understanding Coronary Heart Disease

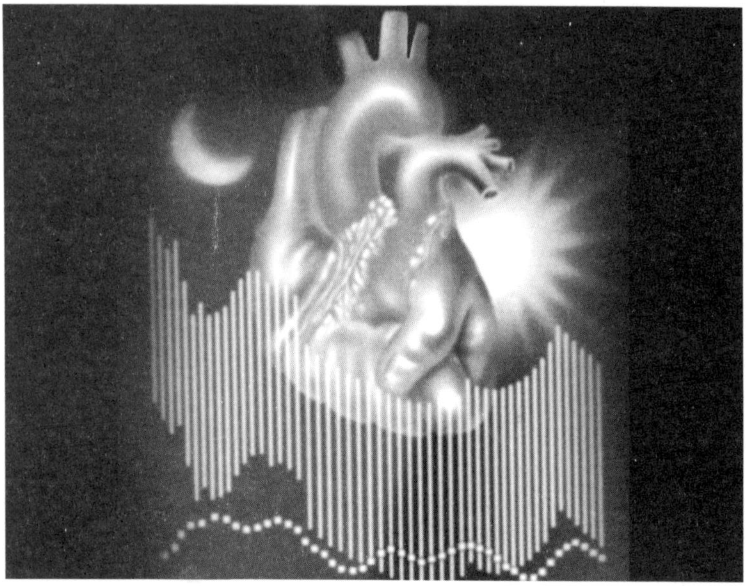

Pumping zestfully with astonishing clockwork precision, at an average rate of 70 beats a minute, over a hundred thousand times a day—the human heart is an incredible piece of creation. Just the size of a clenched fist, located in the chest, a little to the left of mid-line, it gets active much before we are born. The human embryo is just 23-days old, when the heart begins to beat. From thereon, and till we live, it gets no rest.

A four-chambered pump, actually *two* pumps: one—the left—which pumps five hundred thousand litres of oxygen-laden blood

Measure your health by your sympathy with morning and spring. If there is no response in you to the awakening of nature—if the prospect of an early morning walk does not banish sleep, if the warble of the first bluebird does not thrill you—know that the morning and spring of your life are past. Thus may you feel your pulse.

Henry David Thoreau
Journals

into body's circulation in a day's work, and the other—the right—which moves blood to the lungs for its oxygenation, the heart works awfully hard to sustain life. Hooked to it are thousands of kilometres of piping, the blood vessels, that circulate blood into our entire body.

Much as bioscience has progressed, it has not been able to duplicate the heart. For the past many decades, biomedical scientists have been trying to invent its bionic equivalent, but have not met with success. A true gift of evolution, reinventing it still remains a distant dream.

Coronaries—the heart's lifelines

To carry out its huge responsibility, the heart requires a considerable amount of energy. Its hard-working muscles are nourished by two coronary arteries. Buried in the heart muscles, ramifying the heart with their many branches, the coronaries are like little branching trees with trunks not much larger than the thickness of a pencil. Carrying oxygen and glucose-laden blood, they provide the heart with nourishment.

The coronary arteries work 24×7 mindful of the energy requirement of the heart. If we run, feel excited or nervous, and our heart begins to pound, the arteries expand and increase the blood flow to the heart muscle. Their elasticity allows them to widen and meet the demands of the heart on such occasions efficiently. This energizes the heart to function effectively through all odds and pump tens of times the normal blood through circulation.

When things go wrong

A variety of factors may scheme and plot against the health of coronary arteries. As we grow older, cholesterol begins to deposit on the inner walls of the arteries. This process begins very early in life, while we are still in childhood. Over the years, increasing amount of fat is deposited, making the arteries narrower. This compromises the blood flow through them. The arteries also lose their elasticity, and cannot widen in moments of need.

Eventually, the blood flow in the coronary arteries may become so poor that the heart is unable to perform its normal duties. Increasingly, it finds it hard to cope with any extra workload. If sudden demands are made, such as when physical activity is being performed, or emotions rise, and the heart has to beat more rapidly, it feels anguished.

It soon begins to show. Whenever challenged, the heart transmits its agony in the form of discomfort, tightness, and pain over the middle of the chest. This is its way of telling, 'Enough, I can bear no more.' It often forces the person to stop what he is doing, and take rest. This is the well-known symptom of *angina pectoris.* The heart function reduces until it can cope, and the pain then disappears as adequate oxygen again reaches the heart muscles.

The emergence of angina is a sign of danger. Now, the narrowed main trunk of a coronary artery or its one or more branch runs the risk of being jammed. It may suddenly and completely get choked by a blood clot formed on its roughened wall. Or, a fatty plaque or clot detached from an upper, larger artery may travel to a narrowed tributary, suddenly interrupting its blood flow. When this happens and a coronary artery or its branch suffers a complete shut down, the portion of the heart muscle it feeds, dies.

The seriousness of the damage depends upon the size and position of the blocked artery. The larger the affected artery, and less the supply to that area from other neighbouring arteries (which may have sprung up if the process had been gradual), the greater is the damage suffered by the heart. This is a heart attack, or, as doctors name it, *myocardial infarction.* A major assassin, it claims tens of millions of lives every year and has far-reaching social and economic consequences for the families, society and countries that lose to it.

The rising epidemic

Largely thought to be a problem of the western societies until a few years ago, coronary heart disease is today a number one killer disease over most parts of the globe. On the road to modernization, a large number of people worldwide are trading healthy traditional diets for unhealthy foods, physical jobs for deskbound laziness, the relative calm of the countryside for the stressful city. Changes in the social fabric and new structure of the family, which leave little cushion for an individual's problems and failures, technological advancements such as easy modes of transport, machines and remotes, and increase in smoking, all have come to affect the heart. A major tsunami-like epidemic of coronary heart disease is riding people all over the world.

Over the past three decades, cases of coronary disease in India have risen threefold. Even though the disease is more common among the urban people, rural folks have also had to pay the price of globalisation and rapid development. Today, an estimated 7.6 to 12.6 per cent adults in urban India, and 3.1 to 7.4 per cent in the Indian countryside suffer from coronary heart disease. With the structure of India's age pyramid undergoing a metamorphosis, and more people coming under the age bracket where the disease may strike, the number of coronary patients is growing at a worrying pace. Unless the tide is stemmed, India would soon be the hub of coronary disease. By one estimate, 60 per cent of the world's coronary heart patients shall be those living in India by 2010.

The disease strikes the Indians at a much younger age than in other countries. It is often seen among people who have just crossed their thirties and forties. Nearly 50 per cent of cardiovascular-related deaths in India occur below the age of 70, compared to just 22 per cent in the West.

The disease is also more severe among Indians (and other people of South Asian origin) as compared to people in the West. In India, 54 per cent coronary patients suffer triple (or more) coronary vessel disease. The comparable figure in the West is less than half, at 21 per cent. Also, Indian patients have a more diffused form of disease: the length of coronary vessel affected is longer as compared to the Westerners. This makes the job of cardiologists and heart surgeons more difficult.

The risk factors

Over the past five decades, the world community has been making intense efforts to identify the risk factors of coronary heart disease. This has brought substantive evidence to light, and has helped shape preventive strategies.

Smoking

Smoking increases the risk of coronary disease in a major way. The relationship is dose-dependent. The more cigarettes one smokes, the higher is the risk. The risk of heart disease increases by three-to-fivefold in people who smoke 20 cigarettes a day as compared to non-smokers. The risk does not decrease if you use filtered cigarettes or *beedis*, but multiplies several times if you also suffer from diabetes or high blood pressure. Women who take oral contraceptives and smoke also run a serious risk. Even exposure to environmental tobacco smoke, or passive smoking is hazardous to the coronary tree. The risk has been calculated to be as high as 20 to 30 per cent.

Many chemicals in cigarette smoke are toxic to the heart. They cause narrowing of the coronary arteries, reduce the oxygen-carrying capacity of blood and at the same time, increase the workload of the heart by increasing the heart rate and enhancing the resistance to the flow of blood.

By increasing the stickiness of platelet cells and increasing the level of fibrinogen in the blood, cigarette smoking also enhances the risk of clot formation and heart attack. It increases the oxidized bad cholesterol—low-density lipoprotein (LDL)—in the body and lowers the good cholesterol, high-density lipoprotein (HDL). The risk of sudden death is also high for cigarette smokers. The risk relates to release of increased amounts of adrenaline, which can disrupt the heart rhythm.

Blood cholesterol and triglycerides

Having too much cholesterol in the blood is unhealthy. It can lead to harmful deposits in the arteries. The biggest culprit is the LDL cholesterol. It causes not only deposition of fat on the wall of the artery, but also sets into motion the chronic inflammatory process that damages the artery.

The relationship of HDL cholesterol with heart disease is however more favourable. In fact, it plays a pivotal role in fighting heart disease. It cleans the arteries of fat plaques. Doctors therefore recommend that you should pay sufficient attention to it. Too little of HDL cholesterol in the blood can be as bad as too much of LDL cholesterol.

High levels of triglyceride in the blood also work against the health of coronary arteries. Chemically, triglycerides are nothing but fatty esters synthesized by the liver from surplus calories. If one takes too much carbohydrates and alcohol the body has a surfeit of triglycerides.

Medical laboratories do a detailed blood workup of lipid profile, and measure the cholesterol fractions and triglycerides.

Check out: How good are your lipid numbers

Test	Healthy (mg/dl)	Borderline (mg/dl)	Unhealthy (mg/dl)
Total cholesterol	Less than 180	180-240	More than 240
LDL cholesterol	Less than 100	100-150	More than 150
Triglyceride	Less than 150	150-400	More than 400
HDL cholesterol	More than 45	35-45	Less than 35

High blood pressure

Uncontrolled high blood pressure also increases the risk of coronary heart disease. The danger is dual: there is increased hardening and fat deposition in the coronary arteries, and at the same time, because of hypertrophy of the heart muscle, the heart's oxygen demand also goes up. The risk is proportionate to the rise in blood pressure, and is significantly reduced, if the blood pressure is controlled.

Rate your blood pressure (for adults 18 years or older)

Condition	*Systolic (mm Hg)*	*Diastolic (mm Hg)*
Optimal	Less than 120	Less than 80
High normal	120-139	80-89
High blood pressure		
Stage 1	140-159	90-99
Stage 2	160 or more	100 or more

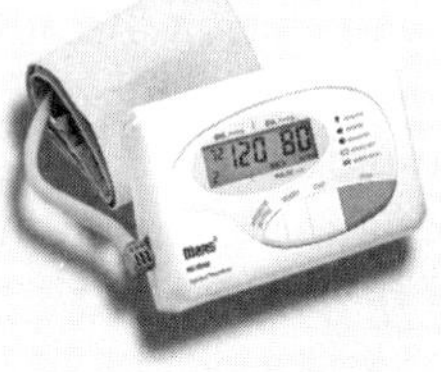

Diabetes

Diabetes increases the risk of coronary heart disease by derailing the body's biochemistry. The risk increases by two times for men, and four times for women. The higher risk in women relates to the end of the natural protection that women normally have during their pre-menopausal life.

Diabetics also run a higher risk of complications following a heart attack. The results of coronary angioplasty are also not very encouraging. A good control over diabetes is your best guarantee against the risk.

Obesity

With obesity, the risk rises in direct relation to the degree of overweight, but it also relates to the distribution of weight. People who carry most of their weight around their waists are often referred to as 'apples'. Those who carry most of their weight below their waist, around their hips and thighs, are known as 'pears'. Generally, it is better to have a pear shape than an apple shape. Fat accumulation around your waist is associated with an increased risk of coronary heart disease.

To determine whether you are carrying too much weight around your abdomen, measure your waist circumference. Find the highest point on each of your hipbones and measure across your abdomen just above those highest points. A measurement of more than 40 inches in men and 35 inches in women signifies increased risk to the heart.

Physical inactivity

If you are a couch potato, you not only run the risk of developing obesity, high blood pressure, and diabetes, you are also at a higher risk to develop coronary heart disease. A sedentary life roughly doubles the risk. Physical inactivity also makes a person more susceptible to sudden death from a heart attack.

Syndrome X

A unique metabolic syndrome, called syndrome X, may play a significant role in the causation of coronary disease in Indians. The syndrome is marked by the inability of insulin to do its job, a rise in insulin and triglyceride levels, high blood pressure and too much weight around the abdomen.

The current theory is that this syndrome may be the result of a thrift gene generated during the course of evolution due to frequent famines in the region. Because of it, the body uses the calories miserly. Now, when the food is surplus, the gene becomes a liability. There is little that you can do about it, except to wait for natural relief. In time, another genetic evolution may undo the risk.

Lipoprotein (a)

Due to genetic reasons, South Asians tend to have higher levels of lipoprotein (a), which increases the risk of coronary heart disease by causing a more rapid formation of fat plaques in the arteries. The risk of clot formation and heart attacks is also higher.

Emotional stress

The mind-body connection is inseparable. There is a valid clinical impression that emotional stress and anxiety are associated with precipitation of coronary heart disease and sudden death. Heart attacks are frequently preceded by phases of acute mental stress. Frustration at work and/or at home is a frequent forerunner of such dismal events. Surgeon John Hunter illustrated the potential seriousness of emotional upset when he said, "My life is in the hands of any rascal who chooses to annoy or tease me." His assessment turned out to be true—he had a fatal heart attack following an argument at a hospital board meeting.

People who are too aggressive, extremely competitive, and hostile towards others appear to be at the greatest risk. Loneliness, major depression and loss of hope can also sometimes tilt the balance in favour of heart disease.

Newer discoveries

In recent years, some researchers have focussed on the possibility of coronary heart disease being of infectious origin. There is some evidence that a common bacterium, *Chlamydia pneumoniae*, may be at play in genetically predisposed people.

The theory of free radicals has also been doing the rounds. Free radicals are unstable molecules with an extra electron that can directly injure the blood vessel wall, induce platelet aggregation, and cause spasm in the blood vessel. Based on these observations, physicians have been recommending a diet rich in vitamins C and E, because of their anti-oxidant properties.

Modest increase in risk of coronary heart disease has also been blamed on elevated plasma levels of homocysteine. Correction of nutritional deficiency of folic acid, vitamins B_6 and B_{12} may reduce the risk.

Unmodifiable risk factors

Age and sex : The risk of coronary heart disease increases sharply with age. Being a man also increases your risk.

Family history of premature heart disease : If you come from a family, where premature coronary heart disease has been common, your risk of developing the disease increases. The risk is compounded if both parents are afflicted with the disease.

Know your risk score

Based on data from the Framingham Heart Study, researchers have devised risk assessment tools that estimate 10-year risk for 'hard' coronary heart disease outcomes. The logic is simple: with each risk factor, the chances of having a heart attack or dying of heart disease over the next 10 years increase. You can estimate the risk for yourself by adding up your score.

If you are a man:

- Do you smoke? No = 0 Yes = 3
- Find your systolic blood pressure and circle the points directly below.

Blood pressure	100	110	120	130	140	150	160	170	180	190	200
Points	1	2	4	5	6	7	8	9	10	12	13

- Do you have diabetes? No = 0 Yes = 3
- Does your ECG show left ventricular hypertrophy? No = 0 Yes =2
- Circle the number where your age and blood cholesterol level meet:

Total cholesterol (mg/dl) / Age (in years)	40	50	60	70
165	4	12	18	21
180	5	13	19	21
195	7	14	19	21
210	8	15	20	21
225	9	16	20	22
240	11	17	21	22
255	12	18	22	22
270	13	19	22	23
285	15	20	23	23
300	16	21	24	23
315	17	22	24	23

If you are a woman:

- Do you smoke? No = 0 Yes = 1
- Find your systolic blood pressure and circle the points directly below.

Blood pressure	100	110	120	130	140	150	160	170	180	190	200
Points	1	2	3	4	5	6	7	8	9	10	11

- Do you have diabetes? No = 0 Yes = 6
- Does your ECG show left ventricular hypertrophy? No = 0 Yes =4
- Circle the number where your age and blood cholesterol level meet:

Total cholesterol (mg/dl)	Age (in years)	40	50	60	70
	165	4	12	18	23
	180	5	13	19	23
	195	5	13	19	23
	210	6	14	20	24
	225	7	15	20	24
	240	8	15	21	24
	255	8	16	21	25
	270	9	16	22	25
	285	10	17	22	25
	300	11	18	23	25
	315	11	18	23	26

Sum up your risk score

Cigarette smoking ☐
Systolic blood pressure ☐
Diabetes ☐
ECG ☐
Age/blood cholesterol ☐
Sex (Male= 5 Female= 0) ☐
Total points ☐

Know your 10-year risk of having heart disease

Total points	Chances (%)	Total points	Chances (%)	Total points	Chances (%)	Total points	Chances (%)
1-10	<1	28	8	36	19	44	39
11-13	1	29	9	37	21	45	42
14-17	2	30	10	38	24	46	46
18-21	3	31	11	39	26	47	49
22-23	4	32	13	40	28	48	52
24	5	33	14	41	31	49	55
25-26	6	34	16	42	34		
27	7	35	17	43	36		

Measures to take

Risk score	Measures
10-20%	Your risk of heart attack is increased, but not yet high. You should have a medical examination and review your individual risk every two to five years. You can reduce your risk by modifying your lifestyle, in particular stop smoking, proper intake of nutrition with use of natural foods, avoidance or correction of overweight, and sufficient daily physical activity.
>20%	You are at a high risk of heart attack. You probably need treatment. Even if you are not aware of any signs indicating heart disease or vascular disease, you should contact a physician to discuss which measures should be taken to prevent a heart attack. You will certainly profit from a healthy diet and a heart-healthy lifestyle (by curbing smoking, avoidance or correction of overweight, and sufficient daily physical activity). In addition, you probably need drug treatment to lower the blood lipids, treat a diabetes mellitus or lower a high blood pressure. You should have your risk factors determined every three to six months. The treatment you receive must be efficient enough to reduce your calculated 10-year heart attack risk below 20 per cent.

Avert the Danger

Mantras for a Rosy Heart

The noblest science of all is the art of living. It affects the quality of each day, the rags and riches of life, and its existing and future joys. Its details are worthy of contemplation for every man. Keeping one's heart in pink of health is inexorably woven into that. If you eat right, exercise regularly, practise moderation in life, control your biochemistry, and do not let stress win, the ticker can beat in tune with life. The benefit would accrue even if deposition of fat has begun in the arteries. In fact, even if you have coronary heart disease, you can profit. Here's what you can do to reduce your risk:

He had had much experience of physicians, and said, "The only way to keep your health is to eat what you don't want, drink what you don't like, and do what you'd rather not."

Mark Twain
Following the Equator

Stop smoking

If you smoke, the risk of heart disease rockets. In spite of knowing this fact, if you keep on smoking, it is like committing a slow suicide. The time to stop is now! Once you quit, the risk of heart disease begins to drop, and by the end of the second year, it is reduced to nil.

The key to stopping is commitment. You may find it hard to keep away from lady nicotine at first because of its firm hold on you, but if you are steadfast in your vow, you can stop. Millions of people have succeeded in their resolve.

Eat right

A healthier diet can carry you to good health. It can help control cholesterol, triglycerides, diabetes, blood pressure, and allow you to reduce your weight. Let us see how:

Eat to live. Watch your calories. Whatever excess calories you take are converted by the liver into cholesterol and triglycerides. This raises the LDL cholesterol.

If you wish to shed those extra pounds around the waist, then you need to curtail the calories. It is a proven formula.

Avoid fried foods. Deep-fried foods, such as *puri*, *paratha*, *pakoras*, *samosa*, *dalmoth*, *mathri*, *bhatura*, *cheela*, *papdi*, *vada*, *dosa*, and *uttapam* are high in calories and fat content. They may please the palate, but ruin the waistline and lipid numbers.

Steam, bake and grill. If you like to cook, it is time to turn to a cookbook that offers recipes on how to steam, boil, grill and bake foods and still turn them into palate-ticklers.

Junk food is bad. Pizzas, hamburgers, triple sandwiches, French fries, potato chips, cutlets and most other convenient carry-away foods are particularly bad. A single medium-sized pizza has 1,400 calories, plenty of fat (the numbers depend on the toppings you choose) and very little vitamins and minerals.

Use healthy vegetable oils. Vegetable oils high on mono unsaturated fatty acids (MUFA) and poly unsaturated fatty acids (PUFA) make a better choice as a cooking medium. Use a mix of safflower oil, sunflower oil, olive oil, wheat germ oil, corn oil, groundnut oil, and mustard oil. Restrict the daily ration to three or four spoons of oil.

Put a stop to using *vanaspati ghee*, or hydrogenated oil. It has the trans fatty acids which increase the LDL. The worst may be coconut and palm oil. Repeated heating of foods also causes hydrogenation of safe cooking oils, and renders them chemically as bad as hydrogenated oil.

Stress on natural foods. Water-soluble fibre, found in whole grains, legumes, fruits, leafy vegetables, and psyllium, binds cholesterol in the intestines and reduces its absorption. Natural food thus helps lower the LDL cholesterol, and at the same time, provides the necessary vitamins and minerals. Foods rich in vitamin C, vitamin E, carotenoids, flavines and selenium also work as anti-oxidants and reduce the deposition of cholesterol in the arteries.

Salads and fruits make the best snacks. If you like to snack, try salads and fresh fruits. Spiced cucumber, carrots, tomatoes, lettuce, cabbage and fruits taste wonderful and are also a source of good nutrition. *Dal bhujiya*, *samosas*, bread *pakoras*, patties, cookies, pastries and cakes are simply passé.

Sugar is bad. Give your sugary tooth a rest. Sweetsmeats (*mithai*), desserts, milk pudding, honey, jam, chocolates, *chutneys,* sweet potatoes, and maple sugar carry a high burden of calories.

Switch to low-fat dairy products. Dairy products are high on 'hard' or saturated animal fats. Butter, scum of the milk *(malai)*, *desi ghee*, and cheese are the worst culprits. The best choice is to shift to fat-free toned milk. To make a clean shift, move to fat-free yoghurt and cottage cheese. Cut down on condensed milk, ice cream, cream dressings, butter and *ghee*.

Restrict meat, poultry and eggs. Meat, especially organ meat, sausages, lard, poultry and egg-yolk have high cholesterol content, and are therefore best eaten sparingly. Lean meat, egg-white and poultry without skin make the best choice.

Fish is rich. All white fish—cod, mackerel, and salmon—contain rich amounts of omega-3 polyunsaturated fatty acids. Regular fish eaters, who take 200-400 grams of white fish every week tend to have healthier levels of HDL cholesterol, and are at a lower risk of developing coronary disease.

Use alliums. Regular intake of alliums—ginger, onion and garlic—holds several health benefits. These foods lower LDL cholesterol and triglycerides, increase HDL cholesterol, and reduce the stickiness of platelets. They also help reduce the blood pressure. Garlic also causes dilatation of the arteries.

Restrict alcohol. Tipplers generally believe that alcohol is good for the heart, but there is clear evidence that it must be taken in moderation. Men must limit consumption to no more than two drinks per day, and women should consume no more than one per day. Excess drinking causes an unhealthy rise in triglycerides and blood pressure.

Get moving

A brisk walk, 30 to 60 minutes each day, can help you attain the fitness level associated with a longer, more healthful life. Regular exercise most days of the week reduces risk of death from all causes, including heart disease, by about three-quarters. The benefits of exercise include the following:

♥ Exercise increases your heart's ability to pump blood and decreases your resting heart rate. Your heart can pump more blood with less effort.

♥ Exercise improves the heart's circulation. It promotes the growth of new collateral blood vessels in the coronary tree, thus maintaining the blood flow to the heart muscle.

♥ Exercise improves cholesterol levels. While it increases the healthful HDL cholesterol, it helps reduce the LDL cholesterol and triglycerides.

♥ Exercise can lower your blood sugar and blood pressure and is especially helpful if you have type-2 diabetes or mild hypertension. Regular exercise also can help prevent diabetes as well as high blood pressure.

♥ Regular exercise improves the strength of your bones and muscles, relieves stress, promotes overall sense of well-being, helps you sleep better and improves your concentration.

How much is good

By gradually increasing the amount of exercise you do, and allowing the adaptive processes to occur, you can improve your fitness level in eight to 12 weeks. To condition your heart and lungs safely, plan well.

See your doctor. If your age is 35 or more, or you have a family history of heart disease or chronic health problem, check with your doctor before starting.

To extract the maximum health benefit, exercise does not necessarily have to be intense. Even walking slowly can lower your risk of heart disease.

Faster, farther or more frequent walking however offers greater health benefits. To help you find out the healthful range of exercise intensity, you can use a simple tool: take a *talk test.* It is simple. While you walk, you should be able to carry on a conversation with a companion. If you can't, you are probably pushing too hard. Slow down.

Frequency: Walk at least three times a week, but if you do it every day, it is best. For conditioning and health benefits, you must in due course aim at walking three to four hours a week.

Duration: Walk for at least 30 minutes. If you have never exercised regularly or have not exercised for a long time, start at a level that's comfortable for you. It may be no more than 10 minutes. Buy a pair of good walking shoes, and begin your journey to good health.

Follow the yogic life

Yoga is an ancient Indian science and way of life. It emanated some 6,000 years ago, and aims at holistic well-being of an individual and progression to a state of perfect bliss. Equipped with a dynamic system of physical exercise, relaxation and meditation, and rich in philosophical thought, it recognizes health at five levels: (i) the physical, or the human body; (ii) the life energy, or *prana*; (iii) the mind, alive with emotions and thoughts; (iv) the higher intellect and knowledge; and (v) the sublime positive energy or *the bliss layer.*

Fundamentally different from the Western school of medicine, yoga strives to impart perfect health. It includes elements that amalgamate to preserve inner harmony. *Asanas* relax and tone the muscles and vitalize the internal organs. *Pranayama* slows breathing and regulates the flow of life force. Meditation calms the mind, and emotion culturing promotes peace and serenity. Regular yoga practice can help reduce anxiety, promote slow breathing, lower blood pressure, alter brain waves and make your heart work more efficiently. On top of all, it just plain makes you feel good!

Control diabetes and blood pressure

Diabetes and high blood pressure are two sworn enemies of the heart. The best strategy to counter the risk is to keep them under control. Bring in suitable changes in your lifestyle. Eat a nutritionally balanced diet by putting emphasis on fruits and vegetables and low-fat dairy foods, restrict salt, maintain proper weight, and exercise. If this does not control them, then follow your doctor's advice: take medication. This can limit the long-term damage that can be caused to your heart, brain, kidneys and eyes.

Reduce stress

Stress is an inescapable element in life. You can fight it and fail, or you may, instead, learn to flow with it. Try and keep a positive outlook towards life, resist frustration, and build rational strategies to dissipate stress. A positive approach, determination, and self-belief are the first prerequisites, but the game plan also includes developing a social support group of family and trusted friends, using appropriate behavioural and mental techniques to relax, and turning to time-tested formulae of exercise, balanced diet, sleep, regular dose of humour, and recreation. Learn to relax. Read a book, play a game of chess, bridge, carrom, or rummy, or take your family out on a picnic. Going for nature walks, enjoying a movie or play, visiting an art gallery, or partying with friends and family can dissipate stress. Even helping your child do a school project or cooking a dish in the kitchen may work out to be an excellent rejuvenator. Your goal is to lower your heart rate, blood pressure and muscle tension, and feel good. If there are any worries, discuss them with a trusted family member or friend. It helps to relieve strains and put things in right perspective.

Medications

There is good data to suggest that the following medications may also lower your risk of heart attack. You can discuss with your doctor how they might fit into lowering your risk.

Aspirin. Aspirin reduces the tendency of blood to clot by weakening the activity of platelets. It is inexpensive, generally safe and easy to take. One baby aspirin (75 mg) taken regularly on a long-term basis reduces the risk of a heart attack substantially. However, you must ask your doctor about its risks and benefits, before starting on it. It is not safe if you suffer from gout, ulcers, blood disorders, or run a risk of haemorrhage.

Cholesterol-lowering medicines. If you have a high LDL cholesterol level, it puts you at risk of heart attack or stroke. To fix this situation, you might consider *statins*—a family of effective cholesterol-lowering medications, under your doctor's supervision. They may be particularly useful if your LDL cholesterol is above 190 mg/dl.

Symptoms and Remedies

All about Angina Pectoris

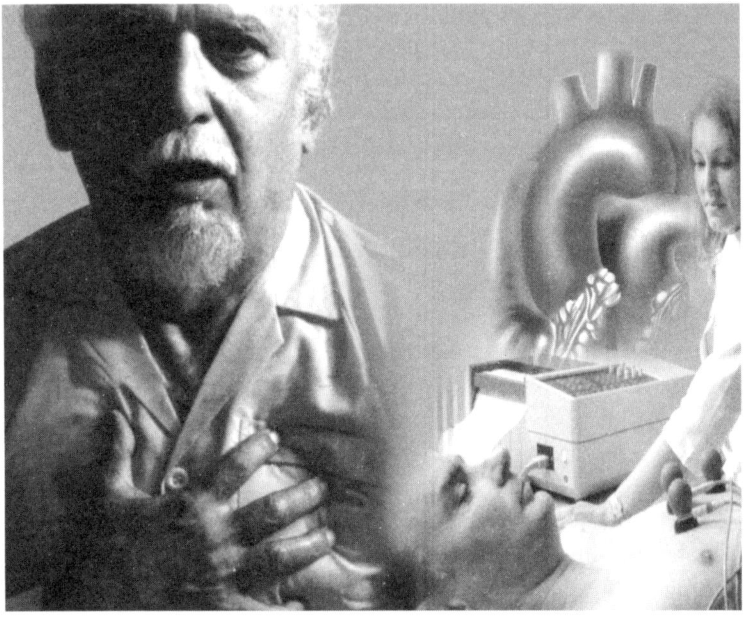

The theme has been exploited for so long by scriptwriters of Bollywood movies and TV serials that any painful or disagreeable sensation in the chest automatically rings a bell of danger in one's mind. Such is its synonymity with heart disease! Yet, it was only at the turn of the 20th century, that the symptom complex was recognized as a part of coronary heart disease.

Much as it may surprise you, angina pectoris is not the name of a disease. Rather, it is the description given to a collection of

People who don't know how to keep themselves healthy
ought to have the decency to get themselves
buried, and not waste time about it.

Henrik Ibsen
When We Dead Awaken

symptoms. The word 'angina' simply means a temporary suffocative attack associated with discomfort or pain. When it occurs in the chest or pectoral region, the condition is called angina pectoris.

Causes

Angina pectoris occurs when the supply of blood to the heart muscles becomes deficient. This generally happens when one or more coronary arteries get narrowed. They are still able to meet the oxygen demands of a resting heart. However, as soon as the workload of the heart increases, the heart begins to feel the pinch of diminished blood flow.

A variety of factors can provoke attacks of angina. They may be sparked off by emotional stress but are more likely to result from physical activities which lumber the heart.

In some people, the pain occurs capriciously without a precipitating factor. The mechanism in these patients is different. The attack stems from a reversible focal spasm in a coronary artery. Such attacks may occur even at rest, and are named variant (Prinzmetal's) angina.

Sometimes, angina occurs as an accompaniment to other heart conditions. A critical narrowing or a regurgitation affecting the aortic valve, syphilitic affection of the great vessel (aorta), and hypertrophic cardiomyopathy which dilates the heart may cause a compromise in coronary blood flow and bring on angina.

Classical symptoms

Classically, angina is a gripping chest pain brought about by physical exertion, anxiety, or other stimuli. The pain is felt beneath the breastbone or in the middle of the chest. From here, it tends to spread over the chest. It may travel to the left and the right (more frequently the left) pectoral region, which is the large muscular region under each nipple. It may continue to spread, upwards into the neck and the shoulders, and down the arms. The left arm is more frequently affected. From the arm, the pain may go down to the elbow, and still further down the inner side of the forearm, often affecting the fingers and the hand. Likewise, from the upper chest region, the pain may spread to the face, involving the cheek and the jaw. Almost invariably, the front part of the chest is involved. But unusually it may be below the chest, in the pit of the stomach.

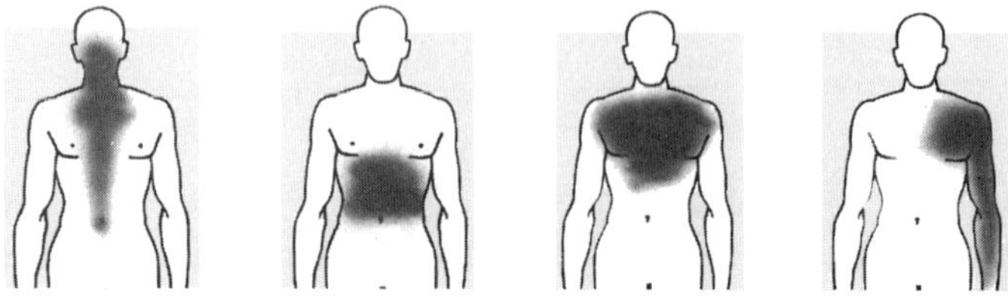

People suffering from angina often describe their pain as vicelike, constricting, crushing, pressing, or a sensation of a weight on the chest. There is no shooting, stabbing or pricking sensation, and the pain is *not* related to the movements of the chest wall that occur during respiration.

Characteristically, the pain usually lasts one to five minutes. As it strikes, the person ceases doing what he is engaged in, and is forced to rest. The pain thus reaches its maximum intensity quickly, and from that critical point, along with the cessation of activity, it subsides, and quietly fades away. The person might also feel breathless.

The commonest precipitating factor is physical activity. It could be in any form: walking–particularly if it is against a wind, uphill or on a full stomach, hurrying, or sexual activity. Anxiety, bad news, argument, anger, fright, frustration, and tensions can also precipitate an attack. The threshold varies by the time of the day and emotional state. A person may report symptoms upon minor exertion in the morning, such as shaving, yet by midday he may be capable of much greater effort without any difficulty.

In some patients, unpleasant, 'energetic' or action-packed, alarming dreams have also been known to produce attacks. It may awaken a person from sleep and be accompanied by palpitations or shortness of breath.

The mimics

Very few conditions can simulate effort angina, that is, chest pain induced by effort and relieved by rest. Most pains related to upper digestive tract, such as indigestion, reflux oesophagitis, with or without a hiatus hernia, could not be effort-related. In any case, the pain in oesophagitis is of a burning nature and is relieved by antacids.

Musculoskeletal pains, particularly those occurring in spondylosis of upper back or neck vertebrae, can be sometimes confusing. They are however not specifically effort-related, and are provoked by specific movements, which angina is not. The pain in costochondritis can be quite awful, but is limited to the junction where ribs and the breastbone meet.

Chronic stress can also tire the muscles in the chest and lead to pain and sense of tightness. However, such a pain is continuous; it is never as brief as anginal pain. Bronchial asthma, when induced by exercise, may also cause tightness in the chest, but it lasts much longer than angina and breathlessness is more prominent.

Diagnosis

A classical clinical history clinches the diagnosis of angina pectoris in most patients. In about half the patients of typical angina, the electrocardiogram (ECG) recorded at rest is normal. A normal ECG therefore does not exclude the diagnosis; however, certain characteristic abnormalities in tracings obtained at rest can confirm the diagnosis.

In cases where the diagnosis is suspect, an exercise ECG (stress test) is carried out. It also has its fallacies. However, when matched with clinical history, its results can be fairly reliable.

A thallium test, can also come useful. It can identify insufficiency in coronary blood flow and the damage caused by a heart attack.

A few patients with chest symptoms without any corroborative evidence from any other quarter may need a coronary angiogram to settle the diagnosis. This test images the coronary tree in actuality. It can thus be used to reliably diagnose and establish the severity of the disease.

Treatment

If you have been diagnosed to have angina, you must not feel depressed. You can still lead a long and useful life. With this positive frame of mind, initiate changes in lifestyle that can stop the progression of disease. At the same time, discuss with your doctor what treatment you would need. Anti-anginal drugs can ease the pain. Some medications also improve the efficiency of the heart. Just in case, you still feel challenged, revascularization measures are at hand to re-establish the blood supply to the heart.

Lifestyle changes

Even if at the cost the repetition, it might help to briefly reconsider the lifestyle changes that might benefit you:

Stop smoking. Cigarette smoking can make the disease worse.

Reduce weight. Dieting to ideal body weight is helpful. If you are overweight, take a diet plan from a dietician and try and achieve the standard weight for your height, age and sex.

Correct the lipid profile. If the LDL cholesterol and triglyceride levels are high, they must be brought down, and HDL cholesterol must be raised to a healthy level. This may require medication.

Control high blood pressure and diabetes. If you have high blood pressure or diabetes, treat them. Lifestyle changes and regular medication can help.

Walk. Unless walking provokes angina, it should help. But before you begin, check with your doctor. By maintaining a good physical condition, your heart becomes more efficient. Avoid isometric exercises such as lifting a suitcase, moving furniture, or pushing a car.

Relax. Avoid circumstances which cause stress, excitement, anger, or frustration. These emotions are punishing for the heart; they push up the heart rate and blood pressure. Be moderate in life and take time off for relaxation, recreation, and sleep.

Do not stress the heart. Do not walk after taking a meal. This can precipitate an attack of angina. If you set out on a cold day, ensure you are adequately clothed. Avoid going on a holiday to hill stations. Reject places which are over 8,000 feet above the sea level, since the atmospheric oxygen becomes rarer at that altitude.

Medications

Nitrates: The oldest anti-anginal pills available, nitrates dilate (widen) the coronary arteries, and improve the blood supply to the heart. They can thus be used to provide relief from an angina attack or to prevent it.

The nitroglycerine tablets are the cheapest. A tablet placed under the tongue, or crunched for more rapid effect, provides rapid relief from angina pain. The effect however lasts for only 20-30 minutes.

A long-acting nitrate such as Isosorbide dinitrate takes more time to be effective than a fast-acting nitrate but it may provide relief for several hours. It may be prescribed as tablets, skin patches, or ointment.

Side effects. Nitrates may cause a pulsating headache, flushing and drop in blood pressure. They are not dangerous or habit forming. However, since they easily go bad on exposure to air, moisture, and sunlight, be sure to cap the bottle after use.

Beta-blocker drugs: The beta-blockers, including Propranolol, Atenolol, Metoprolol, Labetolol and Carvedilol, slow the heart rate, and reduce the force of the heartbeat, thereby reducing the workload for the heart. They also block the action of adrenaline and nor-adrenaline—two chemicals produced by the body that increase heart rate and raise the blood pressure.

Safeguards: Beta-blockers can worsen airway obstruction and must not be used if you suffer from asthma or chronic bronchitis. They can mask the symptoms of low blood sugar, and are therefore not suitable if you are diabetic and take insulin. If you smoke, then also these medications are best avoided, because both smoking and beta-blockers reduce blood flow to the limbs.

Never stop a beta-blocker abruptly. It can cause a hazardous rise in blood pressure, worsening of angina, and increase the risk of a heart attack.

Side effects: If you are taking a beta-blocker, your hands and feet may feel cold since the blood circulation in the extremities is reduced. Some people have difficulty in sleeping. Men may experience impotence, but normal sexual function usually returns when the drug is stopped.

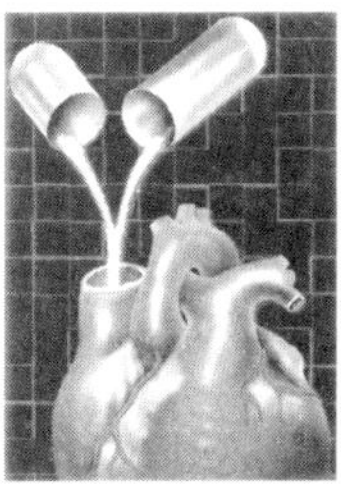

Calcium channel-blocker drugs: Calcium channel-blocker drugs, including Amlodepine, Diltiazem, Felodepine, and Nifedipine, widen the coronary arteries. They are thus extremely useful in the treatment of variant angina caused by coronary artery spasm. Since they also reduce the oxygen demand of the heart, they can benefit patients of chronic stable angina.

Side effects: The most common side effects are headache, light-headedness, flushing, and swollen ankles. Some people also complain of constipation, nausea, palpitations, and excessive tiredness.

Need for angioplasty or surgery

Drug therapy works well in the treatment of angina. Only when it fails, or the disease affects the left main coronary artery stem or three or more coronary vessels critically, there is need to go in for balloon angioplasty or coronary bypass surgery.

Timely Treatment can Save Life

Heart Attack!

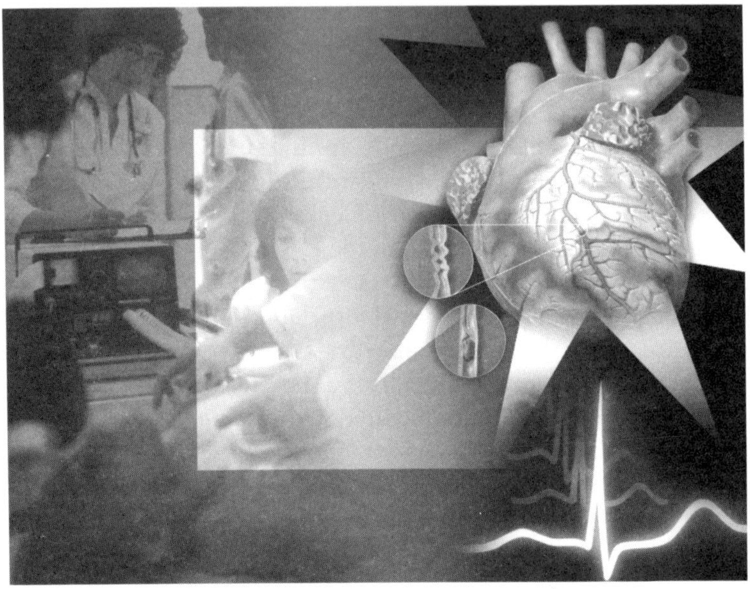

Heart attack! The words quiver with shock. Sending a cold shiver down the spine, they fill you with sudden trepidation. You well realize the danger. Gripping a person within seconds, it can end it all in no time.

A heart attack is a serious event. It requires urgent medical attention. Sensible first-aid can make a decisive difference in the outcome. If the first 60 minutes can be survived, then the outlook improves considerably. However, a close vigil has to be kept for the next 24 hours.

It is a curious sensation: the sort of pain that goes mercifully beyond our powers of feeling. When your heart is broken, your boats are burned: nothing matters any more. It is the end of happiness and the beginning of peace.

George Bernard Shaw
Heartbreak House

The sooner the patient is transported to a coronary care unit the greater are his chances of recovery. A timely shot of clot-dissolving medication can even stop a heart attack in its tracks. Timely therapy with anti-arrhythmic and other medications, emergency pacemaker implantation, mechanical assist devices and cardiac surgery can save life.

What is a heart attack?

A heart attack is usually caused by sudden blockage of a coronary artery by a blood clot. The clot usually forms in an artery that has been narrowed by fatty cholesterol deposits. If the blood flow is blocked long enough in a coronary artery—about 30 minutes to two hours—the portion of the heart muscle that is supplied by that artery will die. The heart muscle death is known as a myocardial infarction; therefore, doctors often refer to it by the acronym, MI.

The blockage in a coronary artery can happen in one of the two ways: in most cases, a blood clot (thrombus) or a ruptured fatty plaque enters a narrowed coronary artery and block if off completely; else, the catastrophe occurs due to a sudden spasm of a coronary artery.

Symptoms

Usually the attack is sudden. One minute the victim is carrying on his usual activities; the next minute he is incapacitated with intense pain which originates in the chest, or sometimes rarely in the pit of the stomach, from where it often travels to the left shoulder and left arm. The patient feels that his chest is being squeezed, constricted, or crushed. The attack may begin under almost any circumstance: while the person is working in his office, attending a luncheon party, driving a car, resting in a chair, or even while sleeping. It may also be triggered by vigorous exercise or àla Mumbai's tinsel world, by an emotional crisis. Often the pain is so intense that there is difficulty in breathing; the person feels weak and dizzy, and may pass out. Frequently, he is nauseated. He often perspires heavily and his skin may turn moist and cold. A feeling of impending death may over power him.

The Danger Signs

- ☛ Uncomfortable pressure, fullness or squeezing pain in the centre of your chest, lasting more than 15 minutes.
- ☛ Pain spreading to your shoulders, neck or arms.
- ☛ Light-headedness, fainting, sweating, nausea or shortness of breath.

You may have all or none of these symptoms, but if you are in doubt, it is best to immediately call your doctor.

The severity of pain differs from that in angina. It increases in intensity until a maximum is reached. There is no let off in the pain with rest. Once having reached its crescendo, an infarct pain usually persists for 30 minutes or more.

The symptoms may however sometimes be confused with those of indigestion, particularly when the pain begins in the upper part of the stomach and is accompanied by nausea. Many instances are recorded where a person has attempted to dismiss his symptoms with a bottle of soda water, a helping of *churan* or a digestive preparation, only to know later that he actually had suffered a heart attack.

In a few patients the classical symptoms do not appear. Some 15 to 20 per cent of myocardial infarcts are completely painless. Their frequency may actually even be higher than this estimate, because without pain, patients are not likely to report to a doctor. Such painless infarcts are more common in patients with diabetes, and their occurrence increases with age. In the elderly, a heart attack may present itself just as a sudden loss of consciousness, sensation of profound weakness, sudden waywardness of heart rhythm, or an unexplained drop in blood pressure.

What to do

If you suspect yourself to be having a heart attack, act immediately. Prompt first-aid may save your life:

♥ Pull all stops. Call for help immediately. If you are alone, call your physician or dial 102 to ask for an ambulance, and state the emergency.

♥ Sit quietly or lie down if you are feeling faint.

♥ Breathe slowly and deeply.

♥ Chew an Aspirin tablet. It thins the blood and improves the outcome significantly.

If you observe someone with chest pain, take the following steps:

♥ Call for medical assistance immediately. If available, a coronary care ambulance may be best. Make the message urgent and clear, stating that the person is having an heart attack.

♥ In towns and cities where facilities for coronary care ambulance do not exist, it is best to rush the patient to the nearest hospital where a cardiologist is available.

♥ While a physician is awaited, make sure that the patient remains absolutely at rest. Prop him up in a half-reclining position. Loosen his clothing. Open all the windows of the room to allow fresh air inside.

♥ If the patient is conscious and a chewable Aspirin tablet is available, ask him to crunch it.

♥ If the person faints or loses consciousness, there is no time to lose. A person at hand or a bystander, who knows how to do a cardio-pulmonary resuscitation (CPR), can still save the situation.

Do's and Don'ts

♥ Make the patient lie down flat on a hard bed or floor.
♥ Raise his legs. This would divert vital blood to his brain.
♥ Take the pillow out from underneath his head.
♥ Start CPR.
♥ Do not try to make the patient sit or stand.
♥ Do not pour water into his mouth.
♥ Do not crowd around the victim.

How to do CPR

If you have been a boy- or girl-cub or a scout, you would probably know how to do CPR. The aim is to keep the airway, breathing and circulation intact, until medical help arrives.

- ♥ Begin by ensuring that the patient's airway is open. Lift up his chin with one hand, and with the other tilt his head backwards. This would open up the airway, relieving it of any obstruction caused by the tongue or epiglottis.
- ♥ Next, move on to breathing. The best way is a mouth-to-mouth respiration. Keep the patient's airway in open position. Pinch his nose, place a fresh handkerchief in between, and give two full breaths

while maintaining an airtight seal with your mouth on his mouth. Look at his chest for simultaneous chest expansion.

- Now, feel for his carotid pulse. It lies in the groove by the side of the Adam's apple. If no pulsation can be felt, begin cardiac massage. For this, locate the notch where the bottom rims of the two halves of the rib cage meet in the middle of the chest. Place the heel of one hand here. Now place your other hand on top of the first one. Bring your shoulders directly over the patient's breastbone and keeping your arms straight, depress it down a good 4 to 5 cm. Then relax the pressure. But do not remove your hands. Compress again. Keep doing this at a rate of 80 to 100 compressions a minute. After every 15 compressions, give two mouth-to-mouth breaths.
- Keep at it, until expert medical assistance arrives. If there is another person at hand, take help.

The next step is to transport the patient safely to the hospital. If the patient is conscious, the doctor may give him a shot of morphine to relieve him of pain and anxiety. He may be administered oxygen, medications to prevent irregularities of heartbeat, and other incidental therapy on the spot.

The first 24 hours of infarction are critical. The biggest danger is from electrical instability of the heart, which can upset its rhythm. If recognized and treated in time, the changes are potentially reversible.

At the hospital

Coronary care unit (CCU)

On reaching the hospital, the patient is quickly transferred to a coronary care unit (CCU), to cope with any emergency. A specially designed nursing unit, equipped to meet all kinds of emergencies in critically sick heart patients, a CCU has a round-the-clock cardiologist, a staff of a highly trained nursing personnel, and a sophisticated monitoring system for the patient.

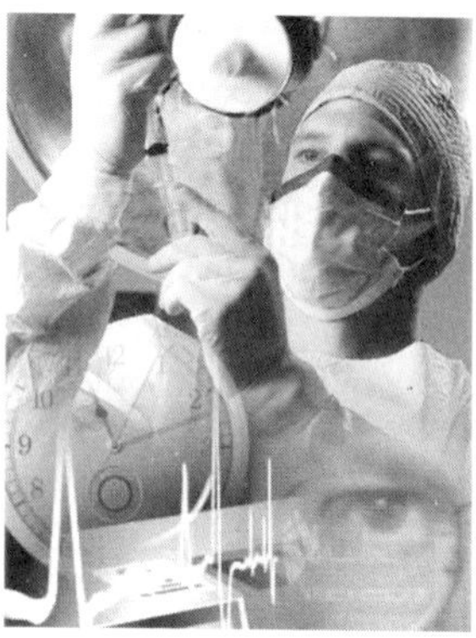

Gadgetry of all kinds—cardiac monitors, defibrillators, respirators, and facilities for introducing pacing catheters and flow-directed balloon-tipped catheters are available to meet emergencies.

Diagnostic tests

The electrocardiogram (ECG) may show the typical changes. Another way is to estimate certain serum heart markers in the blood. These markers (kind of chemicals) are released in large amounts into the circulation from the dying heart muscles affected by the attack. Their time of liberation differs in relation to the occurrence of heart attack. The MB isoenzyme of creatine phosphokinase (CKMB) rises within four to eight hours and generally returns to normal by 48 to 72 hours. However, nowadays the preferred biochemical markers are troponin-T and troponin-I. They are specific to the heart and remain elevated for seven to 14 days after an acute heart attack.

Cardiac imaging also can be a great help. An echocardiography test is a good screening tool. Safe and easy to perform, it can be performed by the bedside of the patient. The test can reveal the extent of damage to the walls of the heart and show the function of the heart. It can guide the doctor in deciding the future course of treatment.

Treatment

The objective of the treatment is to minimize the damage and stabilize the heart. The heart is rested, a close watch is kept on its rhythm and function, and supportive therapy is given as the situation demands.

Thrombolytic treatment

If the patient reaches the hospital within the first few hours, thrombolytic treatment can work magic. Though expensive, it can stop a heart attack in its tracks by dissolving the clot in the coronary artery. This restores blood supply to the heart and saves it from damage.

The biggest limitation with thrombolytic therapy is that it cannot be given to all patients. People with haemophilia or bleeding disorders, those with a history of stroke or any surgery in the immediate past, those suffering from uncontrolled diabetes, high blood pressure, liver or kidney disease, and those who have been administered the medication before, may not be the candidates for this treatment.

Stabilizing the heart

The workload on the heart is reduced by putting the patient under complete bed rest, sedation, and oxygen tent. To maintain the function and rhythm of the heart, he is administered suitable medication. If the heartbeat does not still settle, an emergency pacemaker may be required. In patients whose heart suffers so much damage that it cannot sustain circulation, a mechanical assist device may become necessary. An intra-aortic balloon counter pulsation can tide the crisis.

Emergency surgery

In a few patients, who are in the evolving phase of myocardial infarction and those who suffer from repeated attacks in quick succession, the cardiac surgeon may decide to operate and perform an emergency bypass surgery. The death rate of such surgery is about 4 per cent, but it can prove to be life saving.

Transfer to the ward

The duration of stay in the CCU is dictated by the circumstances. If a patient is doing well and is considered to be at low risk, he may be safely transferred out of the coronary care unit in 24 to 36 hours. On the other hand, if he has a recurrent chest discomfort, suffers a drop in blood pressure, develops a heart rhythm abnormality or heart failure, his intensive care stay is prolonged.

Activity

Any factor that increases the work of the heart during the initial hours of a heart attack may increase the damage. The patient is therefore kept at bed rest for the first 12 hours. However, in the absence of complications, he is encouraged, under supervision, to resume an upright posture by dangling his feet over the side of the bed and sitting in a chair within the first 24 hours. This practice is both psychologically beneficial and usually results in an improved circulation.

If the blood pressure is normal and there are no other complications, by the second or third day he can move in the room with increasing duration and frequency, and may shower or stand at the sink to bathe. By day three or four, he should be able to walk 600 ft at least three times a day.

Diet

In the first four to 12 hours of the attack, the patient is given either nothing or only clear liquids by mouth. Once the condition stabilizes, light food is resumed. The emphasis is on a low-fat, low-cholesterol diet. At first small portions are allowed, and the menu is enriched with foods that are high in potassium, magnesium, and fibre but low in sodium.

Bowels

Bed rest and the effect of painkillers often lead to constipation. A bedside commode rather than a bedpan, a diet rich in bulk, and the routine use of a stool softener are often useful to tide the situation. If the patient still feels constipated, a laxative could help.

The road to recovery

The usual duration of hospital stay for an uncomplicated heart attack is about five days. The remainder of the convalescent phase may be accomplished at home. During the first two weeks, you may increase activity by walking about the house and outdoors in good weather. If all is well, after about two weeks, you can start regular walks on the basis of how much exercise your heart can take. It is also about time when normal sexual activity may be resumed. At this stage, you may return to work. At first, keep a relaxed routine.

Most physicians have a routine of asking you to return four to six weeks after infarction to take the symptom-limited exercise stress test. At the same visit, he may also evaluate your heart's function at rest and during exercise.

In case you suffer angina at relatively low workloads, your heart shows a depressed function (low ejection fraction), or you experience rhythm irregularities on exercise, then you need a further work up and must be extra careful. A cardiac catheterisation with coronary angiography and/or invasive electro-physiologic evaluation can help chart the best possible course of treatment.

Many hospitals also run a cardiac rehabilitation programme for the patients. A progressive exercise plan is initiated in the hospital and continued after discharge. Due emphasis is also placed on improving your lifestyle and taking measures to stop the progression of the disease. A number of medications may also be necessary.

It is natural to feel weak, depressed, anxious and irritable during the first few weeks at home.

However, a healthy, positive attitude, relaxed living with meditation and yoga can improve things. An understanding spouse and a loving caring family can make it easier to cope with the situation.

Some patients may require coronary angioplasty or bypass surgery to return to good health.

Restoring Your Heart's Lifeline

Coronary Angioplasty and Bypass Surgery

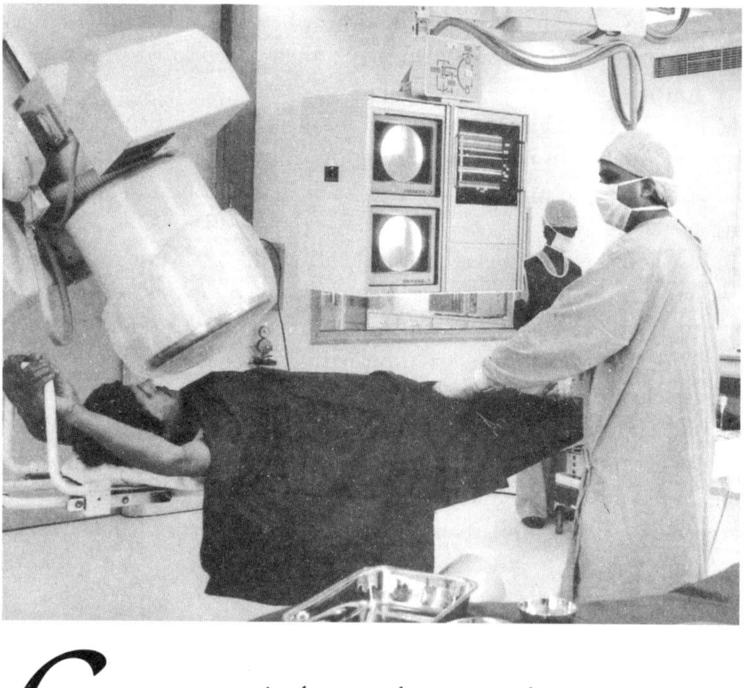

Coronary angioplasty and coronary bypass surgery are two amazing techniques, which work at re-establishing the blood supply of the hardworking heart. They offer a chance of recovery to those patients of coronary heart disease, who find their life severely constrained despite taking anti-anginal pills or who are at serious risk of their life being cut short. Each technique has its own benefits and limitations, and is useful in a definite category of coronary patients.

Life is constantly providing us with new funds, new resources,
even when we are reduced to immobility. In life's ledger
there is no such thing as frozen assets.

Henry Miller
Quiet Days in Clichy

Coronary angioplasty

Beginning as a novel option in 1977, coronary angioplasty has matured into a widely practiced alternative treatment to coronary bypass surgery the world over. The technique uses the simple concept of widening the narrowed coronary arteries to re-establish the normal blood supply of the heart. It does so by using a special balloon catheter, which is deftly manoeuvred into the narrowed or blocked portion of the artery and inflated to clear it of fat deposits. A brief procedure, done under local anaesthesia, it spares the patient a major surgery. In most cases, it only involves one- or two-day hospital stay, and ensures a quick return to normal life.

Who might benefit

Coronary angioplasty is today the preferred treatment for roughly 70 per cent of patients with symptomatic single-vessel disease and roughly 20 per cent of patients with symptomatic three-vessel disease. It has come of age and is being fruitfully used in a wide variety of situations. Even totally blocked coronary arteries can be crossed and dilated effectively. A single procedure can clear multiple lesions. Its use is now no longer restricted to blocks which are close at hand, discrete, and do not occlude the vessel lumen completely.

The use of **coronary stents**—metallic tubes or scaffolds—that are inserted into a diseased vessel segment in their collapsed form and are then expanded to establish a normal-appearing vessel lumen, has made it possible to treat even calcified, or diffuse obstructions in the coronary tree with reasonably good results. Besides correcting constrictions in the native coronary arteries, the technique is also being used to dilate obstructions in bypass grafts. This proves useful to people who have had bypass and again develop angina.

The decision whether to take the patient for angioplasty or bypass surgery is guided by several factors: the accessibility of the narrowed portions, the severity of disease, and the likely benefit that the two procedures might bring. There is evidence to suggest that people with diabetes generally do better with bypass surgery as compared to angioplasty. In all others, the survival figures are matchable, although repeat narrowing(s) are more common following angioplasty.

How it is done

Generally, you are admitted to the hospital a day in advance. You are permitted a light dinner, following which you will be asked to fast till after the procedure is complete the next day. You would be given a medication to help relax before going to bed. The procedure usually takes less than two hours, though it varies with the job at hand.

The procedure is much like a coronary angiogram, and is carried out in the cardiac cath lab. You rest on a motorised X-ray table, and your doctor would be dressed as in the operating room.

You will be given a quick jab of local anaesthesia over the upper leg or groin area. A tiny nick will be made, and a guide wire shall be inserted through the femoral artery, and up into the affected coronary artery. A balloon catheter is passed up the wire, and the balloon is inflated and deflated several times in the narrowed area to widen it. In more than half the patients, a coronary stent is inserted to keep the artery open. This reduces the possibility of the artery collapsing following the removal of balloon. The balloon catheter, having done its job, is then withdrawn.

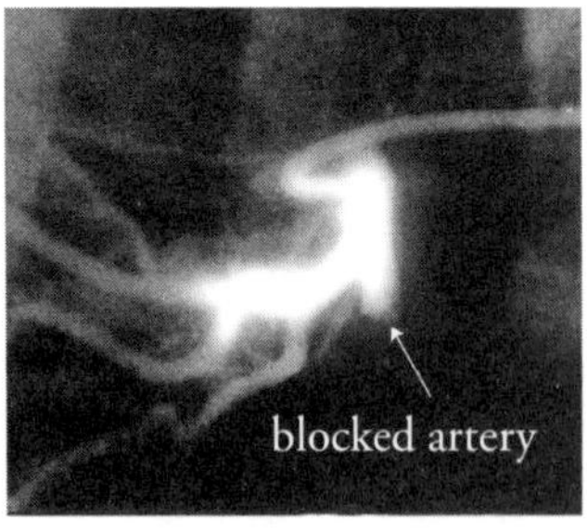

BEFORE TREATMENT

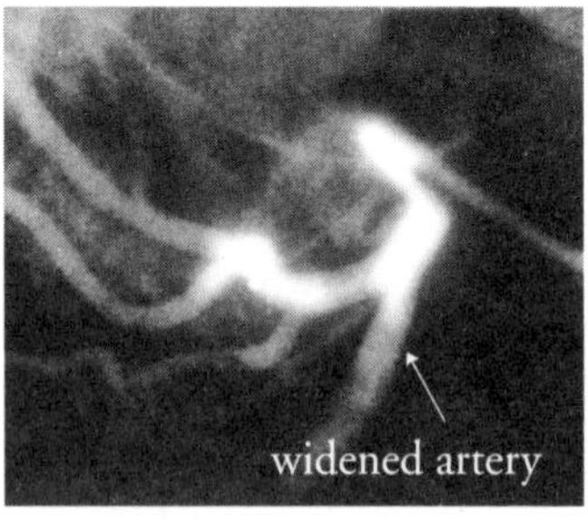

AFTER TREATMENT

Balloon angioplasty: These images show that the blocked coronary artery has been widened successfully and blood flow is re-established.

A set of X-ray images are taken by instilling a contrast dye before and after coronary angioplasty to check if the procedure has been successful.

Aftercare

After the angioplasty is over, you would be taken to the cardiac care unit, where your blood pressure, pulse and ECG would be monitored. You would be asked to hold your leg straight and still for the next six or eight hours. You would also receive blood-thinning medication, vasodilators, and Aspirin to keep the artery open and free of any clots. Once you feel better, and that is usually by the next day, you might receive your discharge slip and go home. Within a week or ten days, you can resume normal activities.

Results

In good hands, coronary angioplasty is a fairly safe and effective procedure. There is, however, a risk of complications, requiring emergency bypass surgery in about one per cent of the cases. A full operating surgical team and an operation theatre is therefore kept in readiness while angioplasty is under way. There is also a small risk of death in 0.4 to 1.0 per cent cases. It must be viewed as an invasive procedure whose risks and benefits for each individual patient need to be weighed before use.

Success rates of angioplasty exceed 95 per cent for dilating a narrowed artery. The follow-up results are however not that good. Roughly 20 per cent of patients develop recurrent symptoms within six months, due to restenosis of the dilated segment. By five years, 40 to 50 per cent will require a repeat angioplasty to maintain an equivalent level of symptom relief.

You must take adequate steps to stop the progression of disease. Curb the risk factors. Remember, angioplasty does not in any way guarantee against the recurrence of disease.

Coronary bypass surgery

A bypass operation offers a new lease of healthier life to the owner of the diseased heart. During the procedure, narrowed sections of the coronary arteries are bypassed by using blood vessels from the leg or chest. The new fuel lines restore normal blood flow to the heart, and thus prevent the symptoms of angina and the risk of heart attack. First carried out in 1967, the surgery is now performed on a regular basis on thousands of coronary patients each year.

Who might benefit

The decision for bypass surgery is usually based on the severity of symptoms, the state of coronary tree, and ventricular function. The ideal candidate is less than 75 years of age, has no other complicating disease, has troublesome or disabling symptoms that are not adequately controlled by medical therapy or does not tolerate medical therapy and wishes to lead a more active life, and has severe narrowing of several coronary arteries. Such patients may achieve considerable symptomatic benefit following the surgery.

The surgery is however not without risk. The risk is more if the heart's left ventricular function is compromised (ejection fraction of less than 40%), if the age is more than 75 years, if diabetes is present, or if the surgery is done as an emergency.

Opinions on whether the surgery helps to extend the life span differ. In fact, results of several studies indicate that bypass surgery probably does not prolong life, unless the disease is severe and the patient has critical narrowing of the left main coronary artery or has three- or two-vessel disease with significant obstruction of the proximal left anterior descending coronary artery.

Preparation for surgery

As is the case of any major chest surgery, it pays to keep your lungs in good health. If the surgery is elective and you have sufficient time, take the following steps.

Stop smoking. In fact, the thumb rule is: do not let anybody smoke in your presence.

Perform deep breathing exercises. The method is simple. Adopt a half sitting position. Place your hands over the upper part of abdomen, just between the angles of the rib cage. Breathe in deep through the nostrils. Next, let the air out slowly with your lips pursed as if you are blowing out a candle. Make sure your shoulders and upper chest remain still, and the hands resting between the angles of the ribs rise on inspiration and fall on expiration. This means you are using your lungs all the way down.

Cough out the lung secretions. Take a deep breath. Hold it. Now, quickly tighten your abdomen and cough the air out, instead of blowing it out. If you do it right, you would feel the stomach muscles contract under your hands. If you just clear your throat, as some people wrongly do, it will not help.

Medications. If you have diabetes, you shall be put on insulin. If you have high blood pressure, adequate measures shall be taken to control your blood pressure.

Surgery

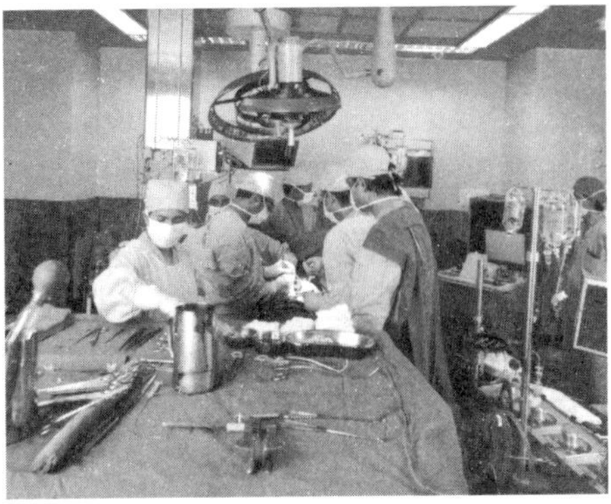

On the previous evening, your body would be shaved, and you would be asked to take a shower. You would be given medication to relieve anxiety and asked to fast after midnight. In the morning, after ablution, you would be given a sedative shot. This shall make you drowsy. You would be shifted on a stretcher trolley to the operation theatre.

Once you are in the operating room, the anaesthesiologist shall stick an intravenous line into you, and he will use it to push the anaesthetic agent. You would immediately fall asleep. The surgery would take between two and four hours.

The surgeon might take two different approaches to access the heart: a midline incision over the chest, and split the breastbone (sternum); or through the left side of the chest. The former approach is preferred if the plan is to perform an open-heart procedure, while the latter is generally taken for beating heart surgery.

Open-heart surgery. In most cases, a heart-lung machine is used to take over the function of the heart. The heart is bathed in a special solution and is stopped. This allows the surgeon to fix the new vessels with ease.

To bypass the obstructed sections of the coronary arteries, he has two alternatives: chip into the internal mammary artery, alter its course and direct it to feed the heart, or construct grafts from the vein drawn from the patient's leg and fix them at one end with the aorta and on the other, beyond the obstructed portion of the blocked coronary arteries. As many grafts as necessary may thus be placed. The heart receives a fresh source of blood supply and you are relieved of the symptoms.

Once this vital part is complete, the heart and lungs are fixed back into active circulation, and the heart resumes its function. The two edges of the breastbone are wired together, and the tissues and the skin on the chest are stitched back.

Beating heart surgery. The second procedure, a less invasive technique, is carried out on the beating heart. The surgeon fixes the grafts while the heart is still active. The procedure is also known as off-pump surgery. It is quicker, and does not usually require blood transfusion.

Post-operative course

Following the surgery, you would be shifted to the Recovery Room, where a team of doctors, nurses, and other trained staff shall provide constant care and monitoring. You might stay in this high care set-up for the next 24 or 48 hours. Once the effects of anaesthesia and medication wear off, you would regain consciousness. However, you might still feel dazed. You would find yourself connected with several wires, tubes and machines. A bedside monitor would continuously monitor your electrocardiogram, heart rate, respiration, and blood oxygen levels. Being sensitive to any change in vital parameters, its warning system begins to beep if it detects any abnormalities.

You may also notice the chest drainage tubes. They remove the bloody fluid from the chest and are connected to vacuum containers placed at the bedside. These drains stay till 24 to 48 hours after surgery. Another tube, the urinary catheter, helps drain urine from the urinary bladder. It is placed into the bladder at the time of surgery. Towards the end of the surgery, the surgeon places two or more pacemaker wires on the surface of the heart. These wires are brought out and stitched to the skin of the chest, and are connected by a cable to a temporary pacemaker box. This standby pacemaker can be used for controlling irregularities of the heart rate and rhythm, were they to occur.

A breathing tube (endotracheal tube) is placed inside the windpipe. It helps you breathe and is connected to a respirator which moves air in and out of the lungs. The respirator is disconnected once you start breathing on your own. The breathing tube is removed a little later, usually 16 to 24 hours after surgery. As long as the breathing tube is inside, it is not possible to talk, eat, or drink. Once it is removed, you might at first feel a little sore in the throat and complain of hoarseness in voice. These effects shall soon wear off. You might also experience mental confusion and encounter weird dreams. These symptoms are transitory and should not evoke concern.

You might still be using an oxygen mask. Intravenous fluids fulfil your nourishment needs. You would be transferred to the intensive care unit for the next few hours, and if all goes well, soon moved to the regular post-operative room. Most of the tubes are out and you are allowed to sit, stand and walk. You should make an effort to continue the deep breathing exercise. You might experience emotional instability—depression, anger, or frustration. It is transitory and it helps to keep one's chin up. By day seven, you are ready to go home.

Return to normal life

You can resume normal activities before long. A moderation of activity and rest is best during the period of convalescence. Initially, getting out of the bed, taking a bath, and dressing yourself may also seem tiring, but as the days pass, things begin to look up.

You must take special care of the incision site. Keep it clean. Wash it gently with soap and water. Report to the surgeon if any redness, swelling, or discharge occurs. The leg incision takes a little longer to heal as compared to the chest incision. You may also see a slight swelling in your ankle. Do not cross your legs. While sitting, keep your legs straight and propped up. Walking is also a good exercise to ease the swelling.

You can gradually resume simple, no-strain activities, such as helping your spouse in laying or clearing the table, or watering the plants. However, you should avoid moving, lifting, pulling or pushing items weighing more than 10 pounds, or vacuum cleaning the house until the next few weeks while the breastbone heals.

You would be asked to pay a return visit to the hospital, usually one or two weeks from the date of release. Now, you would be under the care of a cardiologist, who would monitor your progress, ask for tests to gauge the improvement, and offer you advice about physical activity, medication, and lifestyle.

Sleep a good eight hours at night. A short 15-minute afternoon siesta would be helpful. At about this time, normal sexual activity can also be resumed. A good measure of this is if you can walk three blocks briskly without being tired or short of breath, it is okay.

You may also dine out, go for a movie, or visit friends and family. You can also soon resume work.

Results

The operation is relatively safe, with mortality rates less than one per cent in patients without serious co-morbid disease and normal left ventricular function, when the procedure is performed by an experienced surgical team. Angina is abolished or greatly reduced in approximately 90 per cent of patients following complete revascularization. Within three years however, angina recurs in about one-fourth of the patients but is rarely severe. The outcome is considerably improved by meticulous treatment of risk factors, particularly cholesterol and triglycerides. A healthy lifestyle ensures a healthier life.

Understanding Diagnostic Tests

Check Station

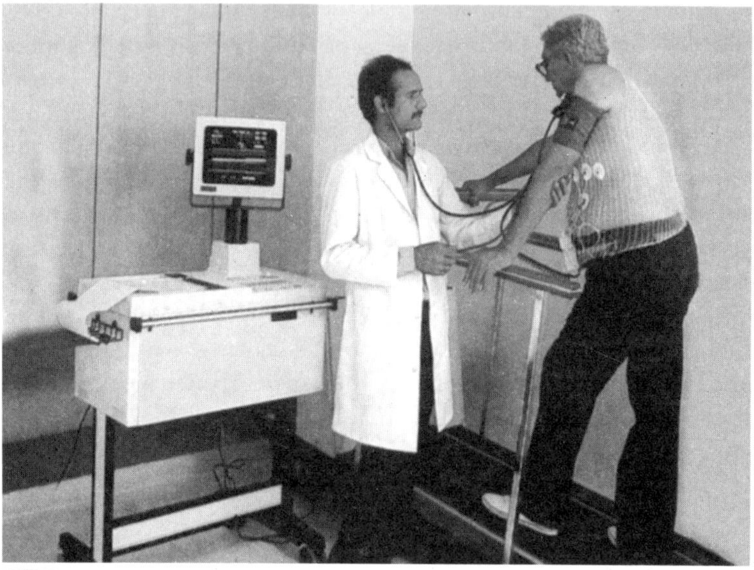

Traditionally, for centuries, *vaids*, *hakims* and physicians had depended on patient's medical history, observation, and examination to diagnose the disease. Stories abound on how the *vaids* perfected the art of reading the pulse. Legend has it that so intense were their observations that they could make the diagnosis by simply picking up the vibrations from a thread tied to the wrist of the patient who rested in another chamber. This remote technique was employed when women of the royal house who practised *purdah* were to be treated.

Among the first diagnostic aids to diagnose the condition of the heart was stethoscope invented in 1816 by the French physician,

There are two kinds of truth: the truth that lights the way and the truth that warms the heart. The first of these is science, and the second is art ...Without art, science would be as useless as a pair of high forceps in the hands of a plumber. Without science, art would become a crude mess of folklore and emotional quackery.

Raymond Chandler
The Notebooks of Raymond Chandler

René Laënnec. The sphygmomanometer, which measures the blood pressure, came next. It was invented by the Italian physician Riva Rocci in 1896. Just seven years later, in 1903, Willem Einthoven developed the first electrocardiograph. Soon, with the advent of many technological advances, newer diagnostic tests came to the fore.

Today, the diagnostic arena in cardiology is replete with a wide array of investigative techniques. Let's take a look at them.

Electrocardiogram

The electrocardiogram (ECG, EKG) is a graphic tracing of the electrical current generated by the heart muscle during a heartbeat. The tracing is recorded with a relatively simple string galvanometer, and it provides information on the condition and performance of the heart.

How it is done: Small electrodes, held with a salt paste, are attached to your chest, wrists, and ankles while you rest on a bed. They lead off the tiny heart current to the recording instrument producing the trace. The test usually takes a few minutes to complete and is safe and painless.

What is its use: The normal ECG shows typical upward and downward deflections that reflect the alternate contraction of the atria (the two upper chambers) and of the ventricles (the two lower chambers) of the heart. The first upward deflection, P, is due to atrial contraction; while the Q, R, S, and T deflections, are all due to the action of the ventricles.

Any deviation from the normal is indicative of a possible heart disorder. Information that can be obtained from an ECG includes whether a patient has suffered an acute or prior heart attack, whether the heart is enlarged and if so, in its which part, whether the heartbeat is irregular, whether a slow heart rate is physiological or caused by heart block, and whether the pericardial covering of the heart is abnormal. An electrocardiogram may also reveal signs of the presence of high blood pressure, thyroid disease, and certain types of nutritional deficiencies.

Stress test

Exercise testing is usually done when coronary heart disease is suspected. The test is specifically designed to evaluate the ability of coronary arteries during conditions of increased workload. The test involves raising your heart rate by exercising and monitoring the heart's function. The exercise is tailored to ensure that your heart is tested adequately without putting you at risk.

How it is done: Small electrodes are attached to your chest. As you exercise on the treadmill or an exercise bicycle, the electric impulses produced by your heart are shown and recorded on an ECG machine. A doctor or a technician keeps a careful watch on your ECG tracing, heart rate, and blood pressure. If you feel discomfort at any stage, or your ECG shows any major change, the test is cut short.

What is its use: A positive stress test is 90 per cent reliable in diagnosing coronary heart disease. If you have had anginal attacks, its positive significance rises further. Still it may be false positive in a few cases. But equally, it may sometimes be falsely negative.

Holter monitoring

A Holter test is a record of your ECG over 24 hours, while you perform your daily routine activities. It is a good measure of what happens to your heart while you walk, climb stairs, eat, watch a movie, play, work, sleep, or make love.

How it is done: You are fitted with a wearable device, the size of a pocket transistor, called the Holter monitor. It records the electrical activity of the heart using a number of electrodes attached to the chest. The device is worn for 24 hours. It also has a button, with which you can mark the time if you face any symptoms.

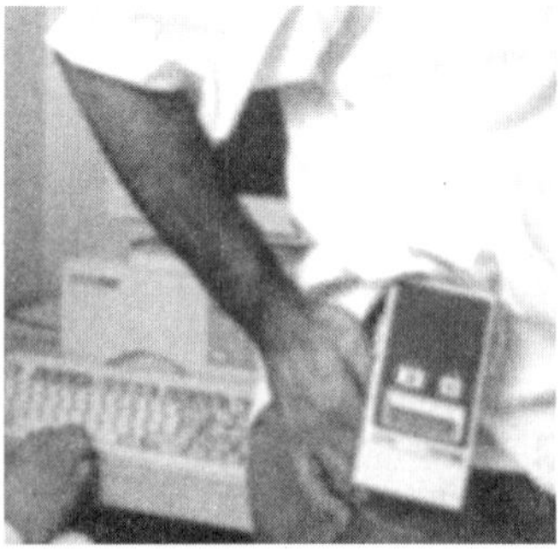

What is its use: The test is of specific value in detecting angina at rest, intermittent arrhythmias (abnormal heart rates and rhythms), spells of dizziness, and to test the usefulness of a medication.

Echocardiography

Echocardiography is a technique that uses ultra high-frequency sound waves to image the interior of the heart. An ultrasound probe, the size of a closed fist, is placed on the chest wall. It emits a short burst of ultrasound waves and then measures the reflection from different heart structures.

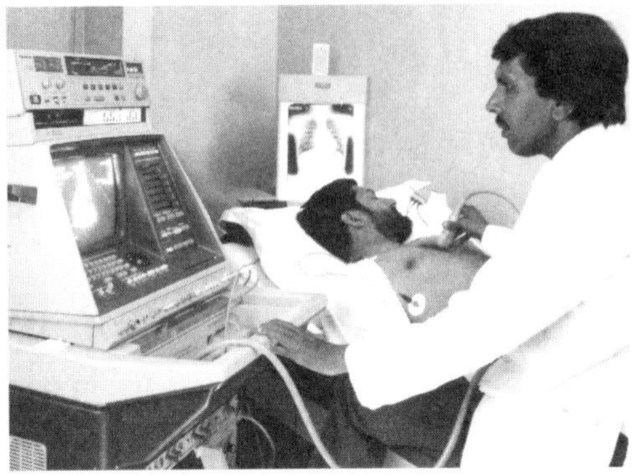

How it is done: You rest on an examination bed. The examining physician applies a gel on the skin of the chest, and a probe is moved over the area. An image of the moving heart is displayed on a monitor screen. It can be recorded on videotape and hard copies can also be obtained. The test usually takes about 15-20 minutes and is absolutely safe and painless.

What is its use: Echocardiography is used to evaluate different cardiac parameters: chamber size, wall thickness, wall motion, valve structure, valve motion, and ejection fraction of the left ventricle. It is the method of choice for detecting diseases of the heart valves, infection of the valves (endocarditis), assessment of left ventricular size, wall thickness and function, identifying aneurysms (a complication of heart attack) of the left ventricle, evaluating fluid collection in the bag of membrane enveloping the heart (pericardial effusion), and a variety of birth heart defects.

Stress echocardiography

Stress echocardiography is another method for evaluating the heart condition when coronary heart disease is suspected. It involves the intravenous injection of the drug Dobutamine, while monitoring the effects using echocardiography. Dobutamine induces the same changes in the heart that would occur during a standard exercise test.

Radio-nuclear tests

Thallium test

The thallium test makes use of radioactive thallium to image the blood flow or perfusion of the heart muscle (myocardium). Injected intravenously, radioactive thallium is rapidly absorbed by the myocardium and is normally

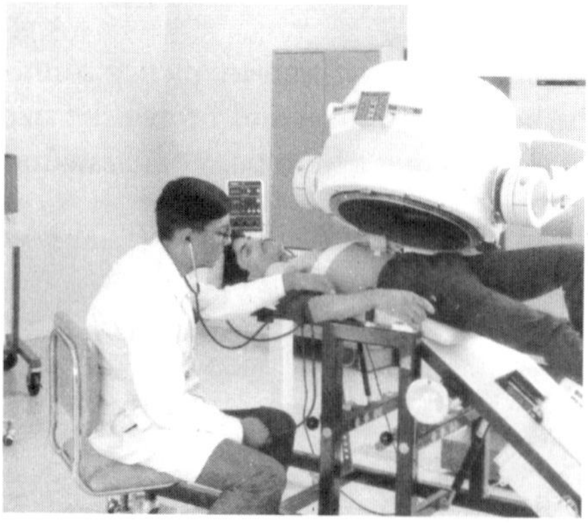

distributed evenly in the heart muscle. Deficient blood flow to a portion of the myocardium is readily detectable by decreased uptake in that area.

How it is done: The test is performed in the cardiac radionuclide lab. You are given a shot of thallium-201, a radio pharmaceutical with special affinity for myocardium. Then the pictures of your heart are taken in different projections using a gamma camera.

Evidence of recent and not-so-recent myocardial infarcts will be visible, but most persons with coronary artery disease who have not had a previous infarction will have normal perfusion patterns when they are at rest. In such a patient, a **thallium stress test** is performed in which the substance is injected while the individual is exercising so that areas of transient ischaemia can be identified. If required, repeat scans are taken several hours later.

What is its use: This test is used to diagnose coronary heart disease. It is particularly useful in patients who have atypical chest pain and their exercise electrocardiogram is non-diagnostic or cannot be interpreted due to one or the other reason. It can also diagnose recent or old heart attack by picking acute infarcts or old scars in the tissues of the heart muscle.

MUGA test

The MUGA test, also called radionuclide ventriculography (RVG), uses a radioactive blood tracer— usually technetium 99m—to delineate the heart chambers and great vessels. The test allows for a reliable estimation of the chamber volumes, left and right ventricular function (ejection fractions), and rates of chamber ejection and filling.

How it is done: The test is performed in the cardiac radionuclide lab. You receive an intravenous injection of a radionuclide into the vein, and a scintillation camera tracks its transit through your right heart, lungs, and left heart. Counts are recorded from several hundred heart cycles following uniform distribution of radiotracer throughout the blood pool. Based on the data, a computer is used to provide images, and various parameters of the heart are calculated. Repeat scans can be obtained up to 20 hours after injection, permitting effects of exercise and medication on ventricular function.

What is its use: MUGA test is most helpful in diagnosing coronary heart disease. It can reliably assess the left and right ventricular functions, and the damage that may have occurred from a heart attack, thereby, prognosticating the patient's heart condition.

Coronary angiography

Coronary angiography is used to image the arteries that supply the heart muscle with blood. The test employs pushing radio-opaque iodinated fluid into the coronary tree, and taking its serial images or a video film on a specialized X-ray unit.

How to prepare for the test: You have to be admitted to the hospital a day in advance. The doctor would do a thorough physical checkup and ask for routine blood work. A small area in the upper thigh would be shaved before you go to bed. You would stay fasting after midnight. On the morning of the test, you may be given a sedative so that you feel relaxed.

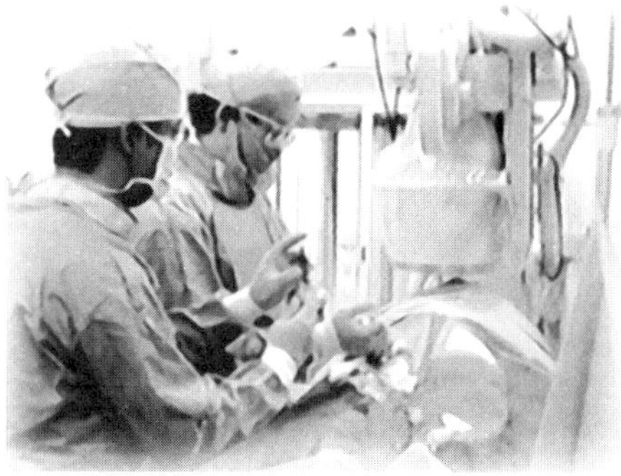

How it is done: The environment in the coronary angiography room is much like that in an operation theatre. Throughout the test, you shall stay awake and rest on an X-ray table. A local anaesthesia is injected, and a fine flexible, catheter is passed into the femoral artery by making a small puncture in the groin. The catheter is passed through the aorta, and is eventually positioned so that its tip rests in a coronary artery. The radio-opaque dye is then injected through the catheter. With the use of X-ray, the dye can be seen to flow easily through the healthy sections but narrows to a trickle where lesions, such as fatty deposits, line and obstruct the lumen of coronary vessels. Cine pictures are taken. Images of each coronary artery are obtained by repositioning the catheter and injecting the dye. Once the job is completed, the catheter is withdrawn and the puncture site is dressed. You are wheeled out and taken to an observation unit, where a close watch is kept over you for the next few hours.

Risks: The risk of the procedure is small, but real. There is an overall mortality rate of 1 in 1,000. Complications also rarely occur. One in 1,000 people may suffer a heart attack or stroke, and fewer than 1 in 100 patients experience other problems, such as transient heart rhythm abnormalities or bruising or bleeding at the catheter insertion site. Some people also suffer reactions to the iodine-containing radio-opaque dye.

What is its use : Coronary angiography is the gold standard for imaging the coronary arteries. Its great value lies in the diagnosis and exact estimation of the coronary heart disease. It is also a necessary prerequisite for coronary bypass surgery.